No Lines in Nature

Joe Enns

Title: No lines in nature / Joe Enns
Names: Enns, Joe, author
Description: Poems

ISBN: 978-1-0692999-0-1 (hardcover)
ISBN: 978-1-0692999-1-8 (paperback)
ISBN: 978-1-0692999-2-5 (ebook)

Designed By: Joe Enns
Cover Art: Joe Enns

Website: ennsjoe.com

JOE ENNS
ARTS
ENNSJOE.COM

CONTENTS

Blank Scales

BLANK SCALES

1.
My fisheries instructor wears a patch
like a band aid behind his ear
for sea sickness, his finger shoved
down a largescale sucker's throat
to rub pharyngeal teeth.
I'd read of fish in India
with throats so strong,
they crumple a hook like tin foil
and spit it back.

Once a sturgeon spit
my hook back straightened.

The fishing guide pours beer
through the net into the Fraser River
for good luck
up from the Mission Bridge.

We wrap a canvas stretcher
around a white sturgeon
and scan it for tags.
The fishing guide
pulls the puckered mouth
out with a fist,

the sturgeon's fleshy barbel whiskers
that probe silt, sand, gravel, scents,
greasy eulachon spawning beds
now dredged and erased.

2.
At Steveston I wait beside an empty lot
at sunrise as locals walk
along the cannery, now a museum.
The marina store closes next week,
a film of dust on the boxes and shelves.
I buy a brass drain plug
stapled inside a clear plastic packet
opened already.

The estuary commercial sockeye fishery
opens for a day, towering arms
and black circles of nets,
the gaps between dark plumes
of diesel exhaust.

On the survey boat we troll
past the breaker, the buoys,
into the estuary rollers.
Do you get seasick?
they ask me for the tenth time that week.
The captain scans
open water through binoculars,
wind direction and tides.
Whitecaps.

He steers us back up the Fraser
to the marina where the seiners sit idle.

The next day a biologist rocks
awake on the survey boat,
his arms crossed.
The Spirit of British Columbia!
he yawns. The sun glares
on the brown-blue estuary
and the fast backs of porpoises.
Full berths of white ferries face
out from the Tsawwassen terminal,
stacked sea containers under a line
of crane arms on the Deltaport.
Wake washes against a buoy
where a sea lion coughs and flops
into the waves.

3.
In September the pink salmon push
up the Fraser mouth past the Mission
bridge where harbour seal eyes,
round shiny heads bob
at the surface. A seal slips under
and slaps back flippers in the deep water.
I'd often watched seals slap
their back flippers on the top,
then dive under,
rise and slap again,
then back down.

Sockeye stay low to the riverbed,
slower water.
Pink salmon mill
in dense schools with the tides.
Adult salmon don't feed
once they cross the estuary mouth.
They use up stored nutrients,
even resorb the tree ring-like
growth lines on scales.
If you pluck a scale,
it might be blank
like an empty shelf.

4.
Sturgeon have placoid scales,
like sharks, dense like armor
with lines of scutes that dull
with age, scraped along boulders,
logs, riverbed, rusted logging cables.
Scutes are the sharpest on the young.
I once caught a young sturgeon
from shore at sundown
and held the caudal peduncle
with my bare palm to release
it into the silty water,

a cross-hatch of cuts
pulling blood through my skin.

PART OF HISTORY

Mosquitoes cling to the side of his nostril,
but I say nothing. He rubs the knot
in his shoulder and stretches his neck
forward. When Putin invaded Ukraine,
he says, I heard nothing
from my Facebook friends in Russia.
Wars like that are supposed to stay
part of history. They had everything.
McDonald's. Not that that's so great.
He rolls his shoulders and paces.
Last week both my legs cramped
at the same time. He runs both hands
beside his crotch. Right along
both inner thighs. So painful.
I tried to walk it off.

SKIN SALT SYMMETRY

I have Norwegian skin,
she says when I comment
on her tanned shoulders.

My skin browns fast.
The yogurt container cover's
sharp foil rim slices a bloody S

across my index fingertip.
Mosquitoes hone-in on my breath,
the CO2, my body heat.

My family warned me
when I was young
about shaking too much salt

on my corn-on-the-cob.
I ate it, anyway, until I felt sick.
Deep Woods Off numbs my lips.

Wave mosquitoes from my hooded face.
The classic rock station DJs
talk about a girl whose left side

is two inches taller than her right.
Once my heart blipped-out
for a few beats, a brown-out,

and the world cinched to a small circle
like the end of a cartoon
until one big heartbeat

took away my breath
and left a migraine.
My dad's right arm

was longer than his left
from years as a baseball pitcher.
Teal sports tape binds her fingers

to brace her broken knuckle
where she scissored
her middle finger in the gate.

I once licked the blue salt blocks
in the cattle barns as a child.
She holds her phone to my face.

For days I rub my sliced fingertip
skin flap. The penciltip-sized divot
grows over with dust and dirt

and leaves a black scab.
My forearm skin burns,
a peanut butter smell,

as my dark arm hair
bleaches blonde and highlights
the white scar between my knuckles.

It's not enough, she says,
that my knuckle's broken,
but now it's swollen from mosquito bites.

Her black nail polish weathers
to small round patches
in the middle of the nail.

UNTIL IT WORKS

Everyone's winging it.
You sweep topsoil dust
from the fresh sidewalk.
Took months to get concrete.
Regular business
isn't regular anymore.

The wildfire smoke sky
shrouds the warm river
like a cataract. A dead seal
floats with one flipper
raised stiff. Sun-
bleached fur.

The ship's radar cycles
through operating system updates
and won't boot-up. I unplug
and reattach random
cords from the back
until it works.

FEET PER SECOND

I rush to beat the Port Mann bridge traffic
tailgated by a white van covered
in electrician company decals
under a Burnaby sky thick with crows

the new guy grins his chipped tooth
in the office trailer beside the Fraser River
rubs his spider-bitten swollen cheek and jaw
and says things like 'the dad always takes the hit'

my dad once said that we suffer
from time-compression
time quickens as you age

last night I dreamt I time-traveled
to a Netflix *Stranger Things* upside-down world
and tried to evacuate smoke-choked residents
from a Fort Langley senior's home on fire

his greasy palm prints
smudge squashed mosquitoes
on the boat cabin windows
reflecting the light back inside

the boat spotlight catches a rat
that swims in a swirling path
of debris mid-river

I once built from scratch on a breadboard
in an analogue electronics class
a binary calculator and a faulty stopwatch

the Canadian Tire pump-action air rifle
fires at four hundred and ninety feet per second
but the landlord doesn't want the rats to suffer

she smiles her wide gums and tiny teeth
like baby teeth
and says she's only worked on simple linear mixed models
for her master's dissertation on R script

the wifi signal speeds up to three bars
in the corner of the suite near the bed
after the landlord moves the router

sometimes I skim-read or skip sentences
near the end of a book or poem
like a computer grinding code with full memory storage

I watch a baby rat dodge under cars stalled at a stoplight
and the rat emerges lifted away in the beak of a swooping
crow

AFTER THE HEAT DOME

Brown bats tap
          the Fraser at dusk. A beaver
head swirls among rising pink
salmon, dance around deadheads
          that bob like floating faces
          tilted downriver.
Smoke reddens
          the sunset
          behind the Mission bridge,
          cut by a single star.
Black steel
          railway cars sag
          under coal heaps
          at the crossing. The trains
haven't moved for days
          since Lytton burned.

My coworker squeezes
          the red plastic jerry can
          between her thighs,
her bare feet slide
          inside white rubber sandals.
She pokes
          the telescoped and bent
          yellow nozzle
into the generator.
          Don't you think gas
comes out blue?

she asks. Last week
the nozzle flicked gas
in her eye. *Like rainbows*
on water? I ask. *No. It's all blue.*
Gas is all blue.

The Ledcor diesel
tug hums
under the bridge at midnight.
Its spotlight scans
the river and weaves the rippled lights
of Mission: dots above the cottonwoods
that shimmer lines
across the water at an angle.
They tie-off
the empty gravel
barge to a steel
pillar near the shore.
The monolith iron
deck looms
in the dark and swallows
all light and my pupils
dilate.

SLIPPED RIB

We winch the rotator from the river
on your thirtieth birthday. One bolt missing.

Three sea gulls peck at a bloated dead sockeye.
I say that I've maybe thirty years left on earth.

Ugh. You stare at the water,
mouth open. *I'm bored already.*

A flesh-coloured splint encloses your middle finger.
After the x-ray, the doctor said no new bone

grew around the fracture. You need surgery or a bone
graft. Maybe a pin. You eat a lot of calcium.

When you moved out, your father painted your bedroom
black with a massive Batman symbol on the wall.

Last week he sold a first issue of *Deadpool.* Your short shirt
rides up under your lifejacket when you bend over

and exposes a line of lower back skin. I bruise my floating
rib on the metal frame as I unscrew cables.

A half-deflated pink Barbie foil balloon floats past.

The Colour of Hope

PEPPERMINT FRAPPÉ

Last night I watched Carlos Saura's
Peppermint Frappé.
Julián, the balding dentist, clips
magazine ads of female models
and keeps a photograph in his pocket.

On a hike,
I pass a flattened patch
of grey songbird feathers,
like scattered darts or quills
over a wet mosaic of alder leaves.
A dog-dug sand hole mars
the trail where one would
roll an ankle.

Julián fantasizes Elena,
blonde, dressed in white
surrounded by dark men.
She beats a drum during Holy Week
until her hand blisters and scars.
Julián tells Elena the upper

part of the town of Cuenca
is older, and more beautiful,
but everyone lives down below.

Maybe I shouldn't take directions
from the lady with three Pomeranians
in a stroller on the leaf-fallen forest edge.
I find a notched view of the river,
but never reach the hilltop Abby.

Julián remembers The Kneeler,
where he would pray to religious icons
while others spied through the keyhole.
His childhood friend unearths a skull
and remembers a once great dog.

Here barking dogs echo
from unused backyards, moss-
covered brick barbecue
pits and plastic playgrounds,
untarped trampoline frames.

In the film, Elena says that green
is the colour of hope while she sips
the poisoned peppermint frappé.

I'd once obsessed, in high-school
shop class, over a keychain
I made from a magazine cut out:
a woman wading the shallows

in a white bikini with a wide-
brimmed straw hat holding fish nets.
The image blurred
as I soaked the clipping
in epoxy from a syringe
and clamped it between black plexiglass
and clear until it cured, resurrecting
the sharpened ink tincture.

GRAVEL BORDER

Lola puked-up a rock
the other day, my neighbour lady says.
Her golden Labrador—pink handkerchief
around the dog's neck—wags its tail
and drops a smooth baseball-sized
stone on the gravel border
beside my driveway.

I put down my empty recycling bin
and press my hiking boot sole
on top of Lola's rock and she digs
the gravel away in a circle
around my boot. Soon she won't
have any teeth left.

My neighbour wears jogging pants
every day. And sunglasses.
She has two dogs. The other
tawny dog eyeballs
me from the end
of his leash on their shredded,
stone-strewn lawn. His handkerchief
is red and black. He's a rescue
from East L.A.

The tall hedge between our yards
was charred black before
the neighbours moved in.
She says it was arson.
The previous renter burned
their mobile home to the ground
and they rebuilt.

The tawny dog jumps
and barks at me.

He'd appreciate if you didn't look at him.

TAPE ARROWS

You choose the Brazilian Prayer Plant—its red veins and dark green markings, almost neon edges—from the mosaic of house plants next to the motion sensor doors at the entrance to Quality Foods. Retirement-aged people inch by you in the produce section. Two ladies stand and chat—muffled through face masks—in front of the celery and broccoli stand. You wait and then push your cart one row over to the avocados. You turn over an avocado. Do you want one that is ripe now, or one that will be ripe in a week? One lady has stopped chatting and pushes her cart next to yours and stares at you. You look down at the floor; there are no tape arrows. You choose a green—too green—avocado and back your cart away from the lady.

You pivot and push to a side aisle with deli displays of cheesecake and Nanaimo bars. There's a man in a thick winter jacket in front of the mustard rack. His mask has an LED banner where words scroll across. He looks around proudly at everyone and waits for a reaction. You can't read all the words, the only thing you make out is the phrase *Canadian Infidels*. You look back over your shoulder to the produce section where more people have moved in through the entrance. You never got your celery or broccoli.

You wait in the soft drink aisle as a man fumbles a case of bottled water while his wife holds the shopping cart. He glares at you, his face mask crooked on his chin, forehead sweaty. He rushes to get out of your way but drops the case on the floor. He swears. *It's okay*, you say. *I have lots of time. Everything is awkward with covid.* The man and the wife don't hear you because your voice is swallowed up by the fabric over your face.

THE ZIGZAG DANCE

from The Freshwater Fishes of British Columbia J.D. McPhail (2007). Taken from the Life History description of Threespine Stickleback (Gasterosteus aculeatus).

Typically,
the nest has
an anterior and
posterior opening
and is complete when
the male "creeps through"
the nest. This "creeping
through" behaviour signals
the end of the nest-building
phase of reproduction
and the courtship phase.
As nest building nears
completion, males
develop their nuptial
colours and become
very aggressive
in their defense
of the territory
around the
nest site.

When a gravid female
enters a male's territory, he
approaches using a series of zigzag
movements (the zigzag dance). If the
female is receptive, she raises her
head and exposes her distended
belly. If the female enters the
nest, the male rapidly quivers
against her lower flanks and
caudal peduncle. She then
leaves the nest, and the
male immediately drives
her from his territory.
Courtship is not
as stereotypic
as this account
implies. males
spawn with
several
females
before
they
switch
over
to parental
behaviour.

CALL-PLAYBACK

I memorize birdsongs for college
wildlife classes, play twitters
and chirps on random
from an iTunes playlist,
while I commute the Trans-Canada.
I yell, *Great blue heron,*
like a contestant on Beat Shazam
when I hear that low stuttered squawk.

My cousin posts an instagram
story that shows a Paypal
balance screenshot. Seventy-nine
hundred dollars from a thousand
in a couple days from bitcoin.

Ornithologists
use call-playback surveys:
blast taped birdsongs
and wait for answers, note
bearings and distances.
Search for nests.

Field trip at the Seymour
Demonstration Forest.
I sit on a mossy log,
stack of data
sheets, cork boots and yellow
raingear, the red flag waypoint
on my Garmin GPS.
Songs rush, rise
from all directions.
I focus on a thrush,
the notes warble up
at the end,
then another, until the songs
unravel in my head
and I mark
the waterproof paper grid.

My cousin's account DMs
me. *You should try this,*
(italicized red one hundred
underlined twice emoji).
I answer, *How does it work?*
*Message @brandy.br***.*
And tell her I referred you.
But @brandy.br***
is a private account,
a beige-blazered blonde
woman, invisible posts,
a bio that says, *Snipper,*

Day trader
Nothing is impossible
(one hundred emoji).

At home, a song sparrow
calls from inside the fir
hedge as I prune
plum trees. I whistle
back and the sparrow hushes
but flits inside the dense hedge.
Maybe my whistle is low
like a large rival
or an ominous
and confusing voice.

I ignore
my cousin's messages,
but my thumb bumps
the Reels icon and cues
a stream of blooper videos
and I lose an hour
laughing into my palm.

BLUBBER MANE

Lazy sea lions float—dazed and idle—
their flippers up in a wet body raft,
a shameless surrender in the tidal
air. They flaunt their bellies, glutted and fat
on spawned herring, embracing the sea dotted
with gulls between shades that stretch in slats
from the scarred shoreline, crawling with knotted
arbutus pierced with cedars. Water line
shards of kelp and jumbles of clumped, rotted
herring roe. A beached sea lion bull—high-
headed in the night, his throaty barks quake
the quiet coves and scratched-rock cliffs. Moonlight
sparks his blubber mane that shudders and shakes
while window panes shiver and I lie awake.

THE WEIGHT OF WINTER

Snow floats through metal
railing spindles revealing
unseen spiderwebs.

Sagged branches slough snow
in upside-down mushroom clouds.
Spurge laurel leaves wilt.
Waxy Oregon grape blades
stiffen, stretch—expecting spring.

Towering cedar
hedge fortress fails to stifle
swift winter wren trills.

A woodpecker's knock
ricochets from conifer
canopies. Alders
cleave slush-crusted pools where gold
veins pierce the weight of winter.

Snow wafts from cedars
on ocean winds, like a soul
drifts from a body.

TWISTED LEASHES

My right foot cramps at night,
toes point in different directions
and I flatten my metatarsals,
clamped between my hands.
Magnesium vitamins
upset my stomach.

I spray vinegar on the Dragon Tree
potting soil to keep down the gnats.
They buzz my ears as I read.

I dreamt that I lined-up to compete
in a high-level swimming
competition at a drained hotel pool
where the swim lane
was a wet board.
I practiced my strokes
and breath in the chlorine air.

The Lowes cashier logs into the till
and when I hand her a fifty-dollar bill
she says she has no change,
I'm her first customer all day.
But it's the evening.
I know, she says,
it's been that slow all week.

Gnats come out every time
I water the house plants.
They orbit my face
as I write and I grasp
the air with a fist.

Three Labradoodles twist
my elderly neighbour
in their knotted, retractable leashes.
The four-month-old, she says, *is a gift*
from my granddaughter.
She said this could be my last dog.
We can die together.
Oh thanks, a lot, I told her.
We'll both probably only live
another fifteen years.

Plateau Lake Sonnets

GAME-CHANGER

Shrimp pulsed the bare, pale shoal. The white stone
and beaver lodge, the lake edge thick. Sticks
gripped the silt like ribs. Tiny trout pulled lone
threads from my flies and flipped ripples, quick flicks,
near the shore. We shed our coats in the sun
when the wind died and clouds cleared. Reels clicked.
You caught a two-pounder and bonked it. Done.
The body dark and cheeks red. Stomach flat,
spawned-out. You asked, *Would you have kept that one?*
That one weekend you dragged that black Spratley—
the red tail flash—all day. *Game-changer fly*,
you called it. Lodgepole pine and spruce matted
the hills. I switched flies and weighted line.
Slipped the hook low—silent—to a trout's eye.

WATER BOATMEN

That one sundown, I cast a grey Adams
fly with white wings to match the hatch of may-
flies. You gunned the motor every damn
time I settled my line silent and straight.
I'll never catch a fish like this, I thought.
But I stripped my line and it dipped. I played
a thick, silver trout—its stomach stuffed taut
with water boatmen. Blonde bodies and black
lines. On a yellow fly, you sharpied blots
and pushed toothpicks in the sides snapped in half
like legs. *I know evolution isn't true*,
you said, *because cows don't have wings. They can't
be as competitive in nature*. You
cast that sharpied fly—let it rise and swoon.

SMOKE TORNADO

We camped the point. The wind shook our two tents.
Tarps tight between trees—as hung walls—to shield
the fire. Our eyes stung and teared—squinted. Bent
over in our ash-smeared chairs—waved hands—held
our breath. A smoke tornado behind slumped
screens. That one morning in my tent, I peeled
open the flap and watched a young deer jump
through reeds. That one afternoon, near the white
stone—beaver lodge, shadows floated like plump
geese. Closer, we saw a slow swimming line—
of deer heads—antlers and ears. And the trout
were silent earlier when the wind whined,
pushed us in sideways circles, but the clouds
rose and my hook sunk into a trout's mouth.

ONE TIM HORTONS CUP PER HOUR

Your boat leaked—the rough road in, battery
tipped over inside—dripped acid and rotted
the aluminum welds. After forty-
five minutes you trolled up beside. *I've caught*
my limit, you said. *I'm going home*. Soaked
jeans. You zig-zagged the reeds—drifted, knotted—
bail bucket thuds and clunks. Past the white stone
and beaver lodge, the wind wrapped my bow, spun
the boat. The motor leg—dark silt cloud—poked
the shoal. Fly line twisted in the prop—gummed
black grease. Waves pounded the gunwales. The camp-
site, two men beached their boat and said, *Leaks one*
Tim Hortons cup per hour. Idling Dodge Ram
charged their battery with jumper cable clamps.

SAILOR JERRY

Bug spray makes my lips go numb. Face coated
with mosquito clouds and Deep Woods Off.
The bear-clawed bark of birch and aspen grown
through groves of fallen pine piled, bark slumped-off
black like burnt matchsticks. That one clearing, high
voltage power lines. The tapered trail, swath
cut through rolling hills. Clear across this wide
province. That one weekend—Sailor Jerry
in stainless steel mugs. Peeled label backside
pin-up cartoon women tattoos. Carried
Benson & Hedges Gold smokes. We were thread-
bare and foul-lunged. Quit smoking the very
last day, so we didn't come home eyes red,
stumbling, and reeking like complete shit heads.

PERSONAL FLOTATION DEVICE (PFD) PILLOW

That one morning, you leaned against the bow—
a PFD pillow. Your sunglasses
with one lens fallen out on your chest. Now,
one eye clear, the other patched with black glass.
Like a pirate. Half-vision. We re-pegged
the tents twice a day in the wind. *Relax,*
you said, climate change isn't a big
deal. People forget that God could come back
anytime and reset the world. Everything.
That winter, the trout jumped clear of the half-
frozen lake and flopped on the ice. The edge,
a belly boater drifted by and cast
his line on the ice, pulled the trout. He said,
I had to keep them; they were already dead.

RAW HOT DOG WIENER

You bucked-up pine with your chainsaw and cleared
the road through swarms of mosquitoes. That carb
screw needed adjustment because the air
was much thinner there. That weekend you parked
your car in the empty lot at Walmart,
near Gas Alley. The highway after dark,
a man jumped out in front and waved his arms.
I'm not falling for that one, I said. Swerved.
Sped up. That morning you gave me a raw
hot dog wiener from your butcher. *Good served*
cold, you said. But I roasted mine. *Smart plan*,
you said. *That'll bring out the smoke preserves.*
Trout tugged your black leech fly all day. I ran
my grey lead line slow—depths tied to my hand.

BLACK BULLS

That first time. That forestry road. Chevy
Nova fumbled through puddles and boulders.
Roof racks—that fiberglass canoe. Heavy.
The barren campground, those two big black bulls.
Unmoved. Staring. For a week. I tented
the soggy field—beside the wind point—full
of tiny frogs. An amphibious wet
pulse of green with every step. I scraped cow
shit from campfire ring stones, and the trout left
my line alone. Last day, the lake arm shallow.
I fished the shoal, the reeds. Cast a perch flat
fish lure at shadows. And a trout—thick, chrome—
strained the rod while a black bull scratched its back
on a branch—kicked clouds of dust in the grass.

COPPER WIRE RIBS

That one spring, the tackle shop, I needed
flies. The pregnant shrimp, pale beige with orange-dot
bellies, copper wire ribs. The bright red bead
of pumpkin-head leeches. The long, two-pronged
tail of dragonfly nymphs—a plum coloured
thorax like a '52 Buick. Hot,
that one afternoon in the sun. Your burned
skin and blistered hands. *Holy shit*, I said.
You look like you've wandered the desert
for a month. A canoe passed us—two men
paddled fast, lines strained. Later back on shore
they told us, *We tried everything again.*
Tasmanian Devils, but nothing. Sure,
I nodded, but I didn't know those lures.

NUMB FINGERS

When trout take the fly, the line binds—a bent
rod. Strained. We turn the trout's head, and it swims
to us. A slack line. A slipped hook. Half-spent,
the trout sees the boat. I strip the line in—
but not with the reel—silent, tangled coils
pool at my feet. Once I waded the dim
shoal in chest waders, but I sunk in spoiled
silt to my knees. Rotten egg odor rose
from the stirred mud. That one morning, I toiled
the wind, I dragged a big black leech deep, slow.
A monster trout shook my line, its head thrashed—
eye tied to mine and snapped the line clean. Low,
slumped in the wind, my hands shook in my lap,
fingers numb. And what was the point after that?

No Lines in Nature

CIRCULATION

Sleek white grebes
disappear without a ripple,
silent pied divers
in the Fraser River.
Pale changeover cue blips
on a movie screen,
a flutter on the pale
waterline, like the river's
lit from below.

The doctor pulls back the curtain.
Why are you still here?
Sensors taped to my bare chest
on the examination table.
Get dressed. The EKG
on the computer shows
my enlarged valve,
which is normal for men
my size and explains my heart
murmur. Also, I drink
too much coffee.
Two cups per day. Max.
The doctor peers
over the rims
of his glasses.

Broken ice shards
drift under the pier
like a mosaic of bergs,
a moving puzzle.
Two muskrats frolic
and slide across the slabs.
They dive back down
under the nodding water.
I shiver in my North Face
Gore-Tex shell.

Our family line
of lawnchairs beside Lundbom Lake
at sundown. The white crust
saline shore. We eat jubilee
corn on the cob
on orange and yellow floral
pattern plastic plates.
Dad says, *If evolution is true,*
why don't cows have wings?
Wouldn't that be a perfect
advantage? And I can't think
of a reasonable argument
that would not pit
me versus him.

Once I snorkeled a slow,
deep reach of the Okanagan River
above Vaseux Lake
for fish count surveys
and beside my mask
the bank trembled and a cloud
of silt opened up like a pore,
an aperture with the face
of a muskrat that burst
forth and torpedoed
past my fogged mask
like the bank birthed
the muskrat as strands
of milfoil coiled
the snug rubber cuffs
of my drysuit,
my hands swollen
and numb.

BULLDOZER

Cabin cruisers and wakeboard boats
roped to metal stakes line the beach
beside the marshy clearing
where a spike-collared Bullmastiff
watches a woman smoke. She says,
He's just a big bulldozer.

A bearded man tells us he drifts
the lake at night and sleeps
in his red kevlar jet boat.
My boat can take the rocks
and logs, he says.

Small dogs fight
at the crowded boat launch
where a short and shirtless,
hairy-chested, (but bald) man
struts the dock and shouts
orders at his family.

Across Stave Lake the same
lines that etch the cliffs
also extend through standing
dead cedar snags
that jut from the water
around the concrete
BC Hydro station.

PARSNIPS

My grandfather died of parsnips,
he says at Saturday morning coffee.
Put a hole right through his back.
In an oil painting behind him,
a man prays over a loaf of bread.
Also, turnips. Runs his hand
over the thick carpet tablecloth.
They had thirteen kids and then died.
The kids raised themselves.

THE *NOT YET*

1.
I swerve lanes on the 97 south
of Peachland
when my front tire
explodes. I park
on the shoulder
beside Okanagan Lake.
For years I'd pressed
my fingertips between
the tread and said,
There's still more life left.
The spare tire release
is fused and corroded
and rusted iron
flakes fall to my cheeks
and squinted eyes
under the Tacoma bed
as I fray the cable
with bolt cutters. Semis
and cars whoosh
past my legs
stretched along the asphalt
beside the yellow
line. The cable snaps
and the tire drops
to my chest. I'm relieved

the spare still holds air.
Next week I buy
four new BF Goodrich
All-Terrains and I keep
one of the old tires
as a spare, which I ratchet-
strap behind the cab
instead of fixing
the tire holder
under the box
because I procrastinate.

2.
The wind kicks
up on Loon Lake
every afternoon, but the yellow
fourteen-foot aluminum
Mirrocraft stays balanced
in the waves with Dad
steering at the stern
and my weight at the bow. We troll
past the German flag that flaps
over the cabins and Ponderosa pines
at the White Moose
campground. A small rainbow
trout tugs Dad's line,
but his rod curls hard
and tight and the line
strains more than it should.
The line lifts dripping
over the water straight
to the trout speared
in a loon's beak.
Row after it,
Dad yells and turns
an oar to me.
He yanks his line high
over his shoulders until the hook
pops loose. The loon pecks
at the trout behind us.
Why didn't you row?

Dad asks. *Catch*
a loon by paddling backwards?
I ask. *We couldn't catch*
it paddling forwards.
Dad grabs his snapped
line that drifts in the wind.
Well, you could have tried.

3.

Grandpa once had a boat
called the "Not Yet"
and we would laugh
and pronounce it like "Na Chet"
and we would joke that Grandpa's
motors are held
together with clothesline
and vice grips. His boat burst
into flames when he turned
the ignition at the Tsawwassen
marina. He dove
overboard. The charred
fiberglass hull sits on a trailer
chocked on the dusty concrete
floor of Grandpa's shop
beside the potato
sorting machine's zigzag
of conveyor belts. He lies,
coated in soot, inside
his burnt boat and he holds
up a melted lure. *Still good*,
he says and places
it in a Tupperware bin.
He comes in from the shop
and we crack walnuts and watch
hockey in the rec room.

One-by-one,
Grandpa says,
God is taking
my toys away.

4.
Grandpa gives Dad
the Mirrocraft but brings
it up all the time.
How's that boat
working out? Sure is a good
boat I gave you.
Dad rants
about it on the drive home.

5.
Before the boat burns,
I'm small and Grandpa
kicks a bucket
across the boat deck
when I have to go.
I'll hold it.
We cross the saltchuck
from Tsawwassen
until we don't see
any land, just ocean.
Grandpa sets me at the helm,
and I clench the wood
steering wheel while
he drops lines.
He lays down
in the sun and sleeps.
I watch the flat sea horizon.
Maybe we're straight,
maybe we're floating big circles.
Later, Grandpa jolts up
and looks around at the rods
and the water. He holds
a hand up to the sun.

He reels in the lines
and scoots
me from the helm
and throttles up on plane.
He drives a straight line
until we see the shore again.

6.
I'm surprised Dad's
gutted and rusted
camperized bread van still rolls.
I sit on the stained
brown corduroy hand-sewn
driver's seat cushion
and grip the tacky
sun-melted steering wheel.
The bent metal gear
shift stretches up from the floor,
in neutral, beside the motor,
the box hood off,
the engine entwined
in scrap PVC. Dad drives
his backhoe behind
the van and nudges
the van forward.
I can see Dad's face
through the smeared side
mirror. It's the last time
I see Dad drive his backhoe.
When the doctors probed
his stomach tumor,
it bled easy,
and they called
it "angry." Arranging
the rotting vehicles means putting
his affairs in order.

The van jostles
and rolls along the lawn
as wasps circle my face
and bump the windshield.
I spot the flaked paper
nest in a plywood cubby hole
near my head. I lean
away as the van coasts
down the lawn slope
with no brakes and I slam
it into first gear to stop
beside the compost pile.
I jump out the door
and wave wasps
from my face.

7.
Months after the cancer
takes Dad,
Mom and I stare
at the van beside the compost.
That's the worst spot. Mom hires
Kidney Car and they crank
the old van up high
on a flatbed. The van is gone
except for the blue flaked front
bumper that Mom
could craft into a flowerbed
or something.

8.
In Summerland I set
Grandpa's Bradley smoker
outside the sliding glass
door where sugar ants
mill the cracked tile
pressed into the clay
beside the yellow grass.
Dad took Grandpa's smoker
after Grandpa's cancer
and now Dad is gone.
The smoker is like a black
fridge with a thick seasoned
residue coat inside.
The automatic wood puck feeder
on the side slides
in a new wood chip
puck every fifteen minutes.
But the temperature doesn't rise.
I kneel to check the thermostat
knob below the door
and, of course,
the knob falls off.

I unfold my Leatherman
and jab the flathead
screwdriver into the slot,
but yank my hand
back when an electric jolt
snaps my wrist
all the way up
to my elbow.

9.

I drive the forestry roads
between Summerland
and Princeton to Osprey Lake
and sit alone steering
the Mirrocraft at the stern.
The empty bow tilts
up in the air,
and the boat twists
and pivots in the wind
and I'm pushed
into the shallows where reeds
scrape the hull.
At the shore I unstrap
my spare tire from the Tacoma
box and toss
it in the bow for weight,
but the boat isn't level
anymore.

LIVE TRAPS

Fur-bearer traps clutter
the retired Conservation Officer's
basement wood panel walls.
A stop in Princeton on our college
field trip through the Interior.
He fiddles with Conibear
and leg-hold snares,
argues the humaneness
of traps as we take notes.

He signs his self-published
memoir, *All in a Day's*
Work for me and complains
that an editor revised
one chapter in two years,
but sent the book back
and kept the money.
His reflections remind me
of childhood movies
I'm still not over: *The Fox*
and the Hound, *Where the Red*
Fern Grows.

On his trapline the next
morning, we follow him
to the hollowed-out
rotted stump, a dangling
snare. He hides his scent, sneaks
up from behind.
with as few footprints
as possible. He strews
Ponderosa pine needles
on and around the wire-
noose-circled bait.

Once a CO parked
a blue barrel live trap
at my elementary school.
The cougar's ears pinned
back behind the metal
grate door.

Once I visited the Aldergrove
Game Farm and couldn't find
the cougar in its pen.
I stared for a long time.
When I stepped back
from the fence I saw
that the whole time
the cat had sat silent
and camouflaged
right in front of me.

I've never seen a cougar in the forest,
but I'm positive they've watched me.

CHIMNEY-BLOCKED

sunrise adrenaline shit-line up the quarter panel
        from wheelwell to taillights
        white Ford 350 beside Vaseux Lake
headlong sprinting mule deer lopes
        across the highway, smashes the side mirror
        door crumpled
circling turkey vultures
                        vertical
crack in the cliffs across the water

Osoyoos Lake packing boat motor chokes
        engine well oil-streaked pair of stiff sockeye
long crane neck mounted on the dock
        blue plastic totes
        thick brine in the sun,
sockeye sink twitching surrounded by plastic
        eyes bulge at the blank sky
what now? the captain asks
        seine net still strained in the lake
        and the totes full
        fill the boat
dip-netted sockeye slide across the flat floor
carve a shifting line to the dock
        cut over sportfishing lines
        tilt through water-skier wakes

I never went hunting
with your grandfather again,
says my great uncle from Steveston
grandpa wore this high-collared brown jacket
they separated in the bush
and my uncle spotted a deer in a thicket
lined it up in the scope
focused on the ears
but grandpa's coat collar
was the deer's ear

The Richmond fish buyer
at Osoyoos Lake
because the Fraser is closed
cranks the crane controls
stares down at the levers
the crane extended to full height
above the dock
dangles the full tote swinging
dock workers back away
propane forklift parked on the sunbaked
shiny concrete slab
surrounded by clay and drifts
of rolled tumbleweed
years of university
and guess what I'm doing
the metal semi-trailer an oven
in the Okanagan afternoon sun
two-high, chimney-blocked totes
no reefer hum

diesel gauge on empty
a mechanic needs to bleed the lines;
you can't just refill and restart
later the reefer motor coughs
an empty red jerry can
a man thumbs the switch
it was worth a shot
but he'll burn out that ignition

sweat evaporates invisible before it can bead or drip

We map Haynes Creek
an Osoyoos Lake tributary
the dust-dry concrete flume
my naked sun burnt neck
he creek a vein underground now
bare hill wildfire haze highway
switchbacks antelope brush
and the smell of sage
with my boot, I nudge a deer skull
single-tined spiker antlers
the white bone baked
shattered at the nose

WINDFALL

Storm winds scrape the TV antenna on the tin roof.
I climb up and reset so CBC is clear enough

to watch Dr. Zhivago as fire splinters chunks of maple
in the wood stove. I slide open a window enough

to see outside an injured raccoon with one paw flat and raw,
prints through fresh-settled snow. That racoon bold enough,

to be the racoon who stole Twizzlers from me last summer
as I burned windfall. When caught, it clawed high enough

up the cedar tree on layers of shattered shale scoured
from steep mountains. Pressed under ancient glaciers enough

to form a lake and beaches of smooth skipping stones
nestled in a deep valley and settled enough.

FURNACE

1-800-RECYCLE says that Capt'n Crunch
takes all metal now
not just cars
and I mutter, *Holy eff*
when the orange dust
coats my t-shirt
and the wind throws rusted chunks and flakes in my face
when I grunt the corroded cast iron radiator
onto my truck bed and the sun-
bleached,
teal-painted steel furnace panels
still splotched in shredded
fiberglass insulation
skinned in tin foil
behind the shed
where the furnace sits for a decade
or two
after we hoist it from the concrete basement,
the second floor a pine skeleton,
the stairway a gaping hole,
the furnace unhinged and hung
from the rope tight

through the flimsy clothesline
pulley
swings back and
forth
until we drop
it to the bare plywood.

The concrete basement,
the furnace that once roared
next to my weight-lifting bench
and punching bag nailed
to the exposed floor joists above
between spider webs—
ghetto blaster and mixed cassette
tapes,
my recordings of Z95.3's
Top Ten at Ten.
The bookshelf,
a long row of mom's photo albums
numbered in felt pen over the 70s pattern of autumn leaves
across from the deep
freeze
the lid that bangs down when we run
with ice cream
to the light switch at
the stairs

where my sister's obese cat
sits on a pile of moldy
cushions and stares
deep in thought like a cat Buddha.

The magnetic decal of dad's failed
backhoe business
we peel from the furnace panels
and toss
back,
the magnets flopping the sign flat.

And at the Capt'n Crunch weigh scale booth
the woman points to a mountain
of ovens,
washers,
dryers.
I throw the furnace
in pieces on a pile
of microwaves.
A bulldozer roars
past in a flurry of dust.
I say, *I'll be back in a couple hours*
and gesture to the stacks
of car batteries
and empty propane
tanks
There's more where that came from.
And I swerve around
two men in oil-stained jeans

back from lunch
eating their sandwiches
from Ziploc bags
where my pick-up makes ruts
through the massive pothole
half-full of brown water
at the gate in the chain-link fence
topped with coils of razor
wire.

EXPOSURE

Groundwater fills the soil pit halfway. Submerges
golf tees thumbed at the changes in colour.

Hack at a blanket of roots. A frozen salamander
hibernates encased in rotten cedar. I crumble

the wood away from its shrunken body
now open to the winter air. Aspen bark blisters

around the bear claw scratches. We notch
higher with a hatchet—like a bigger bear.

Prince's "Raspberry Beret" on the boat stereo.
I count in the intro, but I mix up my words.

A black and yellow salamander snakes its body
in the rain-swollen river that reaches for the ocean.

Turkey vultures—wings back in a sharp "v"—swoop
down on a riverbank pile of logs. Something dead.

There's something wrong with you, you say when I trip
on riverbank cobble.   I'm heat sick

and palm water to my mouth.

We're hiking in circles,
I say at the stump

with the sun set.   We cut
a hard right through the densest bush   and stumble
        out of the trees
                in the dark   at the road.

Pine needles and cones float   with wood scraps
        over a river back-eddy
                    like solid ground. I step
and plummet.   Icy water

closes around my chest.

NO LINES IN NATURE

Hints of raw umber collect on the heel
of my palm. A wash of solvent and oils
cover an empty canvas—primed linen.
My metal *plein air* easel on a tripod.

This year I watch Rivette's film, *La Belle Noiseuse*, three times.
The old master painter Frenhofer. His wild, grey hair. Blue
shirt. Blue pants. His *atelier* in France—the young model
Marianne poses.

My great grandfather's painting studio:
a greenhouse panel lean-to behind his garage.
He paints an image of two puppies. Oil
on a dried tree bark conk. My birthday present.

My six year old wrists crack when I dive
from the cherry tree—I land on the heels
of my palms in the grass. A sharp pain.
Ear-splitting cry. Hands limp at my chest.

The old master painter—Frenhofer—in the *atelier* in France
says, *It's nothing actually. There's no blood. If I go the whole way,
there's blood on the canvas … On La Belle Noiseuse you see blood.*

Half my scratched marks
will be wrong. Accidents.
The fountain pen, sienna ink. Lines
burst from my fingers. Imagine

the strokes on the canvas before
they become real. Each line
closer to the truth. Rid
the frame of emptiness.

Frenhofer turns over a canvas—a hand limp over a naked torso. Scribbled stomach and shaded breast.

My great grandfather's painting
on canvas, an old man with hands
folded over a loaf of bread.
One hand is missing a finger.

On my canvas, the scratches. The simple
shapes. A *grisaille* layer—greyscale—
to get the values. Dark to light—Paynes Grey,
Titanium White. Strokes are suggestions.

Cherry tree trunk, thick—branches
rotted. Grown since WWII. Dark red
cherries with tiny white worms (fruit flies rise
up from grass). Cherries frozen in ziploc bags.

The young model Marianne—long wavy hair—enters the *atelier* for the first time—high ceilings, skylights, abandoned paintings. *It looks like a church*, she says. Actually, it's an old barn.

I teach myself to paint. YouTube videos.
Magazines. If I could paint the human
figure, I could paint anything. Skin
tone is complicated. Errors are obvious.

Frenhofer and Liz walk across the grass. Liz (wife and previous model) is barefoot and has long straight hair. Frenofer slips his hand down the back pocket of her loose pants. He talks of the model Marianne and says, *She pesters me.* Liz asks, *You mean she's a pest?* And Frenhofer jokes, *Rather nice breast.*

I mow my great grandfather's lawn
once a week for ten dollars. I pick up
fallen apples first—he holds the pruners
on the driveway. Suit pants. Collared shirt.

Vest. Smokes half a White Owl cigar. Ceramic
squirrel ashtray. Reads Dutch books bent
at the table. Talks to me in English,
but accidentally switches to Dutch.

I burn my failed paintings
in the wood stove.
Oil burns very well.

Frenhofer talks of painting Liz for the first time. *I became blind*, he says. *A tactile painting. As if it were my fingers that saw and commanded.*

Up the mountain, an eerie grove
of wind-fallen conifers crisscrossed
and dead snags carved with woodpecker
holes. I look for shapes and angles.

Perspectives. A conk at the base of an alder—
brown folds wrinkled over a white palm. A sword
fern white-washed in raptor droppings
from a flat branch up at a predatory view.

The film *La Belle Noiseuse* is based on a short story by Balzac.
In the story, Frenhofer says: *the human body is not contained within
the limits of a line…A line is a method of expressing the effect of light
upon an object; but there are no lines in Nature, everything is solid.*

An artist on a podcast
says she puts a garbage can
in front of her easel
to force distance.

The chicken barn laying box, a low plywood
box with hen-sized holes and a hinged
lid. A wire mesh bottom suspended
above the dust floor. A fat white hen

avoids the box, lays her eggs in a gap
behind the screen door and pecks
the shit out of me when I toss
her across the barn to grab the eggs.

Liz sits on the outdoor table and sips orange juice and asks Probus the art buyer if she should use arsenic soap to kill insects. He says no, he doesn't want to find her one day with a black tongue. *Why?* she asks. *Because you suck your fingers.*

The first painting I sell—a still
life of a fly fishing rod and reel. Fishing
gear strewn about—lead bouncing betty
weights, copper Colorado spoons. A winter

spent fishing steelhead—spoons with pink
rubber eggs. Minus ten Celsius. Rings
of ice collect on my waders. A bald eagle
shits oily white into the empty pool.

Frenhofer pours wine at the table and the young painter Nicolas says, *For me painting is the stroke. A colour that stands out… Something sharp, finished.*

My brown and white springer spaniel
puppy on the lawn at three
in the morning to pee. Next to the cherry
tree. Noises from my dad's flatbed

trailer. A skunk waddles
between us, tail flared. We freeze
and watch the skunk disappear
under the chicken barn.

Cornstalks piled-up on the silt riverbank.
That beaver drags them over
from the fields every night.
Tail slaps on the water.

Frenhofer tacks up a blank sheet and talks of another artist who did a work called *The Resurrection.* He says, *You get stuck inside what you're searching for. Possession.* Then he stretches out Marianne's arm, crosses her naked legs, and arches her back so that she pushes out her bare chest.

Railroad tracks beside my great grandfather's
house. A straight, flat line. Creosote beams.
Black bodies of garter snakes recoil from foot-
steps. Heads pulled back—mouths open wide.

Frenhofer stands next to an abandoned painting under a skylight and talks of stability as happiness. *By entering the door,* he says, *you've brought trouble, but you too will be unhappy.*

Edges. Hard edges. Soft edges. Missing edges.
Working to focal points. A portrait. Eyes. Nose.
Ear. Necklace. Areas of contrast—sharp colour.
I paint images from my laptop. Pixels.

A sharp-shinned hawk caught
in a white mist net. A bird-banding
volunteer holds it by the talons
and passes to another volunteer,

they accidentally let go
at the same time. The hawk lifts
over their heads—bursts
into the sky—with steady wingbeats.

Young painter Nicolas in the *atelier*. Leans on a post and says that there is silence in the room. Frenhofer disagrees. *Can't you hear the forest? The sound, the sound, the murmuring, all the time. It's like the sea. Just like the sea. It's the fossil sound of the universe. It's the sound of origins. The forest and the sea mixed together. That's what a painting is.*

White hospital bed. Great grandfather—dull clouds
in his eyes. Only Dutch now, we don't understand.
We shift him to a comfortable angle and he grasps
my hand, his life etched in lines on his face.

Why wouldn't a stroke burst the sky? asks Frenhofer.

Dad chases a peacock down the railway
tracks. We follow dad in the blue
Oldsmobile. The peacock waits until dad
reaches it, and then flies away again.

Limited palettes. Three primary
colours. Red. Blue. Yellow. And white
to lighten values. Fewer pigments
suspended in oil unify the painting.

Summer copper pool. A gopher snake
hangs from a branch. Bounces up and down.
Dips its head in the water. Startled,
it falls into the stream and swims away.

In Balzac's story, Frenhofer speaks of Rafael and says, *Every face is a whole world. The subject of the portrait appeared for him bathed in light of a divine vision; it was revealed by an inner voice, the finger of God laid bare the sources of expression in the past of a whole life.*

A skunk wedged under the wire mesh
of the laying box. My dad and the neighbour—
the neighbour's shotgun. I fish
the stiff skunk out with a hockey stick

I snorkel the lake shallows. Abandoned
iron rails. Clay banks. Underwater piles
of stones. Two garter snakes swim. Dull
umber bodies dive and pick out a sculpin.

Pheasant chicks in sawdust under red
heat lamps. Grow to adults in the chicken barn.
Dad doesn't want to butcher them. He chases
them out the screen door into the fields.

The young painter Nicolas holds up the wing of a taxidermy bird on the table for Liz. *Wider.* Liz blows on the breast feathers and cuts with an exacto knife. Liz says, *You're white as a sheet. Even green.* Nicolas walks over to the window and his nose bleeds.

The second painting I sell is a young
rainbow trout underwater. The buyer
says her husband loves fishing. *Is it*
for him? No, she says, *I just like it.*

Helpful rules to oil painting: lean before fat;
thin before thick; fast-drying before slow.
Oil takes a long time to cure. It could settle
into a web of cracks over long periods of time.

Taxidermy class, students clean innards
from dead songbirds—stuff them—insert
wooden tongue depressors. Lined up
like dead bird popsicles.

Probus and Frenhofer argue. Frenhofer says, *The aim of art is not to copy nature, but to express it. You are not a servile copyist, but a poet!…Effects! What are effects but the accidents of life, not life itself? A hand… is not only a part of a body, it is the expression and extension of a thought that must be grasped and rendered.*

At the mouth of the canyon, the river dense
with Chum salmon (green and red blotches on their sides).
Teeth long and crooked. Dad wants a Coho,
yanks his rod at different angles to unhook the Chum.

Yellow light in the chicken barn at night.
Dad snags the moulting, barren chickens
and twists their necks. He drops them trembling
into a wooden frame encased with chicken wire.

We bury the frame in the field.

I shake my waders and bend down to break
up the ice. A camouflaged fisherman hides
in a crevasse in the canyon. His line drifts
far downstream and he hooks a steelhead.

Nicolas asks what *noiseuse* means and Marianne stands on the stairs in the *atelier* and says, I*t's from noise. Nuts. Like going nuts.* Frenhofer agrees. *A pain in the arse,* he says.

The beaver skull from the wetlands.
Bird banding with mist nets: white nets
over grass between shrubs. A chickadee
wrapped tight like a cocoon. *Don't touch*

that bird, the banding leader yells. It's not like
pulling fish from a gill net. I find the beaver
skull in the shallow water, a small hole
at the back, where the bullet entered.

Frenhofer shoves Marianne's naked leg under a stool and says, *I'll break you to pieces…I'll get you out of your body…get you out of your carcass.*

I pull the teeth from the beaver
skull and soak it in diluted bleach.
A strong smell. The skull goes white,
the facial bones more brittle now.

Concrete foundations of houses. Forms.
Wet cement poured between plywood gaps.
A grid of metal bars—waler bars.
I smack the bars with a hammer

to release them. Ankles in mud. A jagged
corner slides between my knuckles—
my blood on the hammer handle.
The white line of a scar.

Frenhofer positions Marianne in a black lawn chair and talks of how he has dislocated models' bones. *Your whole body,* he says, *not just some pieces… I don't care about your breasts, legs, your lips…* He says that he wants everything and will put it into the frame. He arches her naked back from behind and says, *I'll get to know what's inside… under your thin surface…* He ponders and then says, *It's the line, the stroke. Nobody knows what a stroke is.*

My aluminum jar hangs from the *plein air*
easel. Latches jingle when I dip
the paintbrush bristles
up and down in the solvent.

Quail trap. A chicken wire covered frame.
One end a funnel, the other a tunnel
capped with a bucket and a cedar shingle
flap. Birdseed bait. Strewn for a week

under the pines. A bucket-full caught
one morning. The neighbour releases
the small ones. Hammers the heads
of the others. I clean them with scissors.

YouTube tutorial. Snip the neck. Tail. Wings.
Legs. My finger under the skin—releases
from muscle and bone (in one pull). Snip two lines
beside the spine. Breast and legs in my palm.

Frenhofer says that eventually nothing is left of happiness but
a memory. If a chord in their hearts has not been touched,
something will be lacking, a something in the stroke of a
brush, a mysterious element we call poetry.

I hold long brushes by the end
of the handle. Strokes loosen with less
control—expressive. Soft sable
bristles absorb too much. Weak

strokes. I scrape paint on the canvas
with a palette knife. A still
life of a level-wind fishing reel.
Each stroke bound in hard

edges—harsh. I abandon it.

Once finished, Frenhofer covers *La Belle Noiseuse* in a green tarp and buries it in the wall of the *atelier*, cementing it behind a wall of bricks. The corner of the tarp slides up and all you see are the heels of the figure, surrounded in a flash of red.

ACKNOWLEDGEMENTS

This collection of poems was created throughout my studies in the Creative Writing and Journalism program at Vancouver Island University. Very much a period of learning and growth in the complexity of written language, many people helped to shape my poetics throughout this process. These poems are the outcomes of that influence. Sonnet L'Abbé taught many of the poetry courses that blew my mind and pushed me to see things deeper, and I would like to thank Sonnet for the always constructive feedback, long conversations, and friendship. A number of the poems in this collection were also written in courses with Robert Hilles and I would like to thank Robert for the encouragement.

Canadian literary journals were kind enough to publish a number of poems in this collection. My gratitude goes out to *The Dalhousie Review* for publishing "Circulation;" *The Fiddlehead* for publishing "Game-changer" and "Raw hot dog wiener;" *FreeFall Magazine* for publishing "After the Heat Dome;" and *Portal Magazine* for publishing "The weight of winter."

My education and writing practise would not be possible without the support of my partner Kelly Corbett. Kelly is an amazing painter and business woman who has always encouraged me to work towards my life goals while also keeping me grounded. I owe this chapter of my life on Vancouver Island to Kelly and I am grateful every day for our relationship where we both give everything to help the other achieve their creative dreams.

Joe Enns is a fisheries biologist and artist living on Vancouver Island, British Columbia. He's earned a Bachelor's degree in Creative Writing and Journalism from Vancouver Island University, and a Bachelor's degree in Ecological Restoration from the British Columbia Institute of Technology. His poems, nonfiction, and book reviews have been published in literary journals across Canada. *No Lines in Nature* is his first poetry collection.